# Slides and Negatives

## Digitizing and Protecting Your Vintage Film

**Gary W. Clark**

Slides and Negatives:  Digitizing and Protecting Your Vintage Film

Cover and interior design by Gary W. Clark

Edited by Gena Philibert-Ortega

# Acknowledgements

I must thank countless people who I have met over the years, many with the same questions about slides and negatives, and other photography related topics. These people have inspired me to share my 40 years of accumulated knowledge with others.

I was lucky to be surrounded by photographers in the 1970s who influenced my respect for negatives. I still have comb-bound glassine negative books from the era filled with precious negatives, all in perfect shape.

While some storage materials and techniques have changed, the same basic concepts apply: store the negatives and slides in non-destructive materials, and catalog them so they are easy to find.

I also wish to thank many of my ancestors who left me a vast treasure trove of negatives; some from well before World War II. Also, I express gratitude to my dad who documented our family life throughout the 1960s and beyond with thousands of slides.

More recently, I wish to thank Dean Palmer, a cousin with a wonderful collection of vintage slides and negatives, along with scores of century-old cameras. He has generously loaned many pieces for illustration and reference in this book.

Gary W. Clark

# TABLE OF CONTENTS

# INTRODUCTION

Most families have photographic negatives and slides from previous eras; sometimes the collection of negatives outnumbers the printed photographs. While these may seem difficult to view, they can be a blessing. Vintage negatives, even 15 year old film seems vintage, may be found in their original envelopes; therefore, they are not scratched or damaged. Slides are usually in protective boxes or maybe in carousels or slide trays; again protected from mishandling.

While slides and negatives are not as easy to view as printed pictures, they can be turned into fantastic digital images which can then be viewed on a computer, tablet, and through the internet. These same images can be formatted to nearly any size and then printed as photographs on your home printer or at local stores through convenient kiosks or internet uploads.

Negatives and slides should be copied, protected, and archived with as much care as photographs. These original images may be the only source of family images.

This book takes a comprehensive look at four primary areas of interest that will help safeguard your film collection: 1) Archiving your slides and negatives for safe keeping, 2) Cleaning the film, 3) Digitizing the images in optimal formats and size, and 4) Identifying and handling potentially hazardous film.

The time invested in archiving your negatives and slides can provide limitless enjoyment to you and others.

Please safeguard and copy your negatives and slides.

Gary W. Clark
PhotoTree.com

# MATERIALS, SIZES, AND HISTORY

Understanding the types of negatives in your collection is crucial to safe preservation. This is a safety concern as much as an archiving issue. Frequently found in many home collections, some old negatives are unstable and flammable; this book will show how to identify the dangerous ones and how to treat them.

Slides, also called positive transparencies, do not pose any safety hazards, though it is important to understand how to preserve and copy them so the images they represent can last forever.

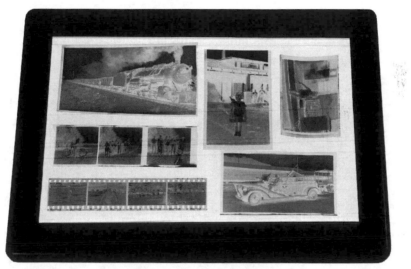

Various size negatives are found in 20th century family collections.

Film collections, whether they are negatives or positives (slides), come in many shapes, sizes, material, and quality. Negatives have been the primary method of capturing an image since the 1860s. Previously, photographs such as tintypes did not use negatives in the photograph process, the image was a direct exposure onto the plate. Tintypes, ambrotypes, and daguerreotypes were one-of-a-kind photographs since there were no negatives used in the process. They can be copied by a camera or scanned, but an exact reprint from an original negative is not possible.

The history of slides and negatives cannot be separated from the history of photographs. The success of photographs from the Civil War era until the 21st century was dependent on negatives. Of course, digital technology has replaced physical film, even though much of digital technology emulates film. The similarities of film and digital are fascinating to life-long photographers, but those topics are for other books.

We will start out covering a short history of film, which will help put your vintage film in historical context, and maybe help you determine its age.

## Wet Plate Glass Negatives

Photographs from the Civil War era, including cartes de visite, cabinet cards, and larger prints were captured on glass negatives. The earliest negatives were called wet plates since the glass was inserted into the camera when the coating and silver nitrate were still wet. These plates were prepared immediately before the picture was taken.

Wet plate glass negatives were coated with emulsion just before the picture was taken. This photograph shows a Civil War era portable darkroom in the back of a wagon. (Library of Congress)

This was not difficult when the photographs were made in a studio, however many battlefield images taken during the Civil War were prepared and taken under difficult conditions.

## Dry Plate Glass Negatives

In the 1870s, a dry plate technique was developed using gelatin as the coating that held the silver solution. This was a tremendous improvement over wet plates as it allowed plates to be prepared ahead of time, eliminating the need to mix chemicals and coat the glass under difficult conditions. This dry technology would eventually evolve into common negatives of the 20th century.

Amateur and professional photographers alike exposed dry plate glass negatives in large box cameras well into the 20th century. The following camera, a Cyclone Sr. by the Western Camera Manufacturing Company was available from 1898 to 1905. It sold for $5.00 and made image exposures on 4" x 5" glass negatives. The 1897 Sears, Roebuck & Co. catalog listed the respected Seed's 4" x 5" glass negatives for 60 cents per dozen.

c. 1898 box camera with 4" x 5" glass negative.

Dry plate glass negatives: from the early 20th century.

Glass negatives presented special problems for photographers. These negatives were heavy, bulky, and easily broken. The required glass was high quality, with no bubbles or other flaws, and therefore expensive. Yet when preserved and stored correctly, glass negatives produce beautiful images. The two plates in the above illustration show the variety of conditions that glass negatives are found. The man's portrait is missing part of the glass and the emulsion is damaged considerably. The negative of the turn-of-the- century (1900) stylish couple on the right was found in its original heavy paper envelope. It produced a quality print as if the picture was recently taken. Scanned images of the negatives are shown below.

Most professional photographers kept negatives on file so they could provide reprints; yet after a year or two, the photographer might wash the image off the glass plate and reuse it.

Scanned glass negatives.

## Glass Negative Preservation

The OCLC (Online Computer Library Connection) WebJunction website has an excellent paper on Preservation of Glass Plate Negatives. If you have a large number of glass negatives, you may find this paper informative and applicable to your collection.

# Flexible Film

The first commercial flexible film (similar to modern film) was introduced in 1889 by George Eastman. This is commonly called nitrate film (nitrocellulose). It is very unstable and highly flammable. Eventually it was replaced by cellulose acetate film that was much safer to use and store. The concern over flammable nitrate film was so high that the newer acetate film was labeled and marketed as safety film. The third type of film base was made from polyester, which is still used today.

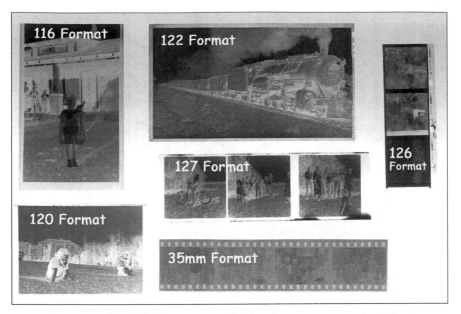

A variety of flexible film were available – largest are usually oldest.

Generally the three types of negative (and film) material were:

- Nitrate Negatives & Film (nitrocellulose)
- Safety Negatives & Film (cellulose acetate)
- Polyester Negatives & Film (polyester)

It is important to understand whether your negatives are nitrate or safety film, which the next chapter explains how to identify each type.

## Transparency Film (Slides)

Also called positives and slides, transparencies became highly popular in the 1960s as a way for a family to share their recent vacation with friends and relatives trapped in a dark room, acting polite as the father advanced his slides and narrated the journey. My father even had the nerve to carry his projector, slides, and screen to other people's houses to share his travelogue.

   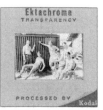

1962                1979                1984           1970 (Ektachrome)

Kodachrome film dominated the slide business.

Kodachrome slide film, immortalized in song by Paul Simon, was introduced in the mid-1930s. The image and dye quality was so superior to
contemporary alternatives that it was a popular film medium until digital
technology overtook most film applications. Many of the memorable photos
from National Geographic Magazine were taken with Kodachrome film.

Ektachrome, introduced in 1946, was a moderately successful alternative to
Kodachrome. The developing process was much simpler which allowed economical processing by amateurs and small labs. Even if not labeled, many
Ektachrome slides are easily identified as the early dyes in the film were not
stable, and images took on a green tint.

## Other Brands and Processors

Film was available from other sources such as Ilford, ANSCO, and Fuji,
though Kodak was the dominate producer. In addition, Sears, 3M, and others entered the film processing business in the late 1950s as the market for
personal photographs was starting to explode.

## Black and White Slides

Slide film can include black and white images also, though they are not
found often. Many black and white slides were produced by amateur
photographers who shot and developed their own film, cut the film, and
mounted their own slides in blank slide mounts. Some slide mounts were
hinged, while others incorporated a slit on one side where the film was
inserted.

Self-mounting slide holders from the 1950s.

## Film Formats and Sizes

Several films sizes were popular throughout the 20th century. Most personal collections will contain one or more of the following:

| Format | Image Size | Used |
| --- | --- | --- |
| 35mm | 24 mm x 36 mm | 1934 - Present |
| 110 | 13 mm x 17 mm | 1972 - c. 2000 |
| 116 | 2 1/4″ x 4 1/4″ | 1899 - 1984 |
| 122 | 3¼″ x 5½″ | 1903 - 1971 |
| 120 | 2 1/4″ x 3 1/4″ | 1901 - Present |
| 126 | 28.5 x 28.5 mm | 1963 - 2008 |
| 127 | 1 5/8″ x 1 5/8″ | 1912 - c. 2000 |
| APS | 17 x 10, 17, 30 mm | 1996 - 2011 |

Note: The image size is the area containing the exposed photo. This is not the physical size of the film.

Many other sizes were available with various levels of use by photographers. You may need to know the format name and size when scanning the negatives or using a commercial service. Appendix A contains a comprehensive list of film formats and sizes.

## Negative Format and Size Guide

A template is available on the PhotoTree.com website, in PDF format, that when printed gives you an easy method to discover the size and format of your negative. Simply match the negative with an outline on the template to identify your negative format and size.

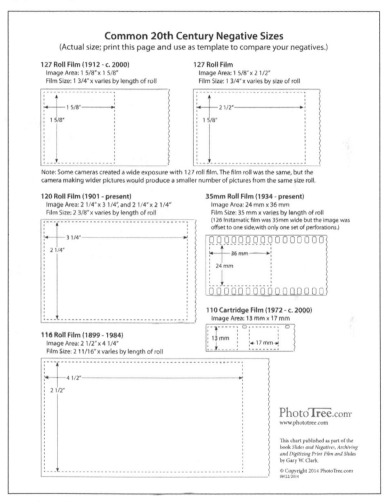

Template download: www.phototree.com/negative_formats.htm.

# HAZARDOUS & SAFETY FILMS

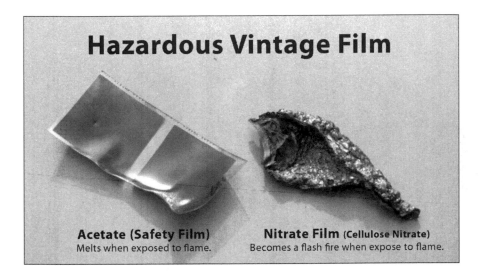

Hazardous Vintage Film

**Acetate (Safety Film)**
Melts when exposed to flame.

**Nitrate Film** (Cellulose Nitrate)
Becomes a flash fire when expose to flame.

Storing older negatives (and movie film) creates some unique and some-time dangerous situations. If you have negatives that were produced before 1951, they may be highly flammable.

## Overview of Hazards

This chapter reveals details of hazardous versus non-hazardous vintage film. However, a short list of issues to be aware of may get your attention and encourage you to read this chapter closely.

- Pre-1951 film negatives may be prone to easy combustion.
- Appropriate storage is the key to preventing a disaster.
- Pre-1950 motion picture film is exceptionally dangerous.
- Post-1950 negatives may deteriorate, but are not dangerous.

Cellulose nitrate film, usually referred to as nitrate film, was produced until 1951. Cellulose acetate, know as Safety Film, replaced nitrate films begin-ning in the late 1940s with complete replacement (in Kodak films) by 1951. Polyester film in turn replaced acetate films beginning in 1960. These materials were used to create the base of the film, with the image residing in the emulsion that coated the base.

| Film Base | Used | Status |
| --- | --- | --- |
| Nitrate | 1890s to 1950 | Flammable |
| Acetate | 1950 to 1960s | Non-Hazardous |
| Polyester | 1960 to Present | Non-Hazardous |

## Identifying Hazardous Film

Sometimes hazardous films are difficult to recognize from non-hazardous. A well-preserved nitrate negative can look the same as a negative made with safety film. Compare them closely using the identification techniques listed in this chapter and try to determine when they were produced.

Generally, you should be aware that any film created before 1951 could be nitrate film and therefore hazardous.

Professional use of nitrate included motion picture, X-Ray, and aerial film. This book is focused on vintage negatives found in the home, though many of the documents referenced in this book also discuss non-consumer applications.

# Nitrate Film: Fire Danger

Much fear has been created about the dangers of nitrate films. While the fire-danger is very real with nitrate films, this is most applicable to film made before 1951.

Nitrate-based flexible film was used almost exclusively in early motion picture film. Dramatic fires have wiped out many commercial motion picture libraries. Early storage practices of movie studios and government archives contributed to the disasters. Large volumes of film kept in airtight metal canisters, in large warehouses with no environmental controls created environments where spontaneous combustion sparked devastating fires.

These threats do not apply to most family collections of photographic negatives, yet dangerous environments must still be avoided.

## Identifying Nitrate Film

Nitrate films give off fumes and an acrid smell similar to camphor when they deteriorate. In addition, their unstable nature causes the film to deteriorate in unfavorable storage conditions such as high temperatures and humidity. Here is a checklist of conditions to look for when determining whether you have nitrate film.

- The edge of the film reads NITRATE.
- For sheet film, the text will be embossed; for motion picture film, the text will be printed.
- Kodak brand sheet film prior to 1940 will have a "V" notch near its upper right corner.[1]

A warning is due however; lack of the above markings is no guarantee the negatives are not nitrate.

The following characteristics were derived from tests conducted by the author, with these films confirmed as nitrate.

- Some films before 1950 have a 'V' exposed along the edge.
- If a negative shows 'silvering', it should be treated as nitrate film. Silvering is an uneven sheen or metallic look to the negative.

"V" Imprinted on Negative
Indicates Nitrate Film

This 127 Format Negative had a series 'V' markings spaced 2.5" apart.
Negative is from 1939, my mother is sitting on the bumper

Even if your film does not have any of the above markings, you may still have nitrate film since a majority of film manufactured before 1950 is nitrate based.

Tip – I have conducted extensive fire tests on negatives from my family collection. All tested negatives prior to 1950 were nitrate film and were extremely combustible, yet most were not marked in any manner.

## Deterioration Characteristics of Nitrate Film

Numerous institutions list different levels of deterioration, each level increasing the hazard nature of nitrate film. (Sometimes Levels are described as Stages of deterioration).

- Level 1 - No deterioration.
- Level 2 - Yellowing and mirroring.
- Level 3 - Sticky and strong noxious odor.
- Level 4 - Amber color and faded image.
- Level 5 - Film is soft and can weld to adjacent items.
- Level 6 - Becomes a brownish acid powder.[2]

Tip – Nitrate films can be preserved or duplicated until the third level of deterioration. Nitrate films that have reached the fourth level or have no historical value, should be destroyed by professional services.[3]

When each successive level is reached the likelihood of fire hazard increases, and precautions should be taken. If your negatives exhibit advanced levels of deterioration, please take recommended actions for disposal.

## Nitrate Film Handling Recommendations

A Kodak guide on nitrate film boldly includes an ominous statement:

*"You must handle unstable or deteriorated nitrate films much like you would explosives".*[4]

This book will not cover all the technical aspects of dealing with nitrate films; the subject is extensive in scope and is covered in the reference material cited in this chapter's endnotes.

Some major points however need to be considered immediately if you suspect there are nitrate negatives in your collection:

- Immediately make high quality digital copies.
- Do not store in high temperature, high humidity environments.
- Use appropriate storage sleeves or envelopes.
- Do not store in sealed containers as this may induce spontaneous combustion.
- Do not mix with other films or documents.
- Do not discard with household or business trash.
- Seek a disposal service for large quantity disposal.

## Motion Picture Film

Early 35mm motion picture film is especially susceptible to fire and spontaneous combustion. This extra danger is caused by the nature of motion picture film being wound in larger rolls containing more film than single photo negatives, and the practice of being stored in airtight canisters that encouraged deterioration, especially when stored in warm environments.

Be extremely vigilant with older motion picture film, and if you discover any film exhibiting deterioration characteristics described in this chapter, seek a professional disposal service immediately.

If your home movie packaging is labeled Safety Film such as the next image, your film is safe, though appropriate storage is recommended.

---

Tip – 16mm Kodak film was never produced using nitrate base. All 16mm film is safety film. 8mm film followed 16mm, and is classified as safety film also.

---

16mm Motion picture film from the 1940s.

## Cellulous Negatives: Safety Film

The hazards of nitrate film were so well known that non-flammable replacement film was called safety film. This terminology was probably a marketing effort to boost confidence and sales of newer film. However, it also helped the photographer and consumer with their storage needs by clearly identifying a safer product.

Tip – A common method of identifying acetate or safety film is to smell it for a strong vinegar-like odor. This is a sign of safety film deterioration, but not a hazard.

Safety Film was printed on some Kodak negatives.

Safety film was made from cellulous acetate, which is stable and not prone to combustion. This film replaced flammable nitrate film by 1951, and was in turn replaced by polyester film in the 1980s.

Not all safety films were labeled like this c. 1953 black and white negative. Kodak labeled many of their films with the notation "Kodak Safety Film" along the edges, however most other manufacturers did not included such labels, even though the film was in fact safety film.

Tip – Even though your film may not be labeled Safety Film, if it is from 1950 or later, it is probably safety film. Examine the film with the nitrate characteristics in mind to be sure.

## Acetate Film Deterioration (mild to worse)

- Level 1 – No deterioration.
- Level 2 – Negative curls and turns red or blue.
- Level 3 – Vinegar smell, shrinks and is brittle.
- Level 4 – Warping.
- Level 5 – Bubbles and crystals.

Even the worst level of safety film deterioration does not create a fire hazard, though early copying or digitalization of the images should be conducted.

Once the deterioration steps have progressed, there is no process to reverse them.

## Disposing Hazardous Nitrate Film

If you have determined your collection includes nitrate films, especially if they have deteriorated, dispose of them in a safe manner. Every city or area will have different services available to dispose of hazardous material, either public or private. Many city or state governments offer hazardous waste removal services.

---

Tip – Search the internet with your favorite search engine (Google, Bing, etc) for "Hazard Waste Material Disposal [your city]" to find a service near you.

---

Do not dispose of hazardous materials yourself. Also:

- Do not mail or ship nitrate films – it is against the law.
- Do not discard nitrate films in household or business trash.
- Do not burn in furnace or closed container.
- Do not store nitrate film in hot, humid environments.
- Do not store nitrate film near a flame or heat source.
- Do not store nitrate film in airtight containers.

If your negative collection includes nitrate film still in good condition, experts recommend that you copy the negatives (high-resolution digital scanning) and then destroy the negatives. Exceptions to destroying nitrate film is frequently granted to historically important film that can be professional stored in climate controlled, environmentally safe conditions. Due to storage and archival costs, these collections are usually found in government archive agencies, museums, or universities.

The decision to dispose of nitrate films is up to the owner. Chapter 3 describes how to store (using glassine envelopes) nitrate negatives that have not deteriorated. However, under no conditions should you keep nitrate film (negatives or motion picture film) that has begun to deteriorate.

# Burn Tests on Vintage Negatives

I have conducted hazard tests on old negatives, and logged, photographed, and captured video images of the tests.

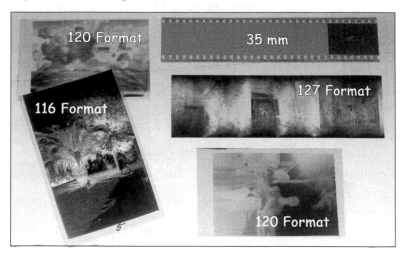

Selection of negatives used for burn tests.

The tests included actual flame tests on vintage negatives. Fortunately, numerous sets of negatives in my collection, from different eras, contained poorly shot images. Some were over-exposed or under-exposed, or very blurry, providing no useful value to family history. However, these poorly-shot negatives became perfect candidates for flame tests to discover, verify, and illustrate the flammability of typical family negatives.

## Do Not Try This

I do not recommend that you try these tests yourself; they were conducted under optimum safety conditions, with great care. However, the images and videos were created to give you a sense of realism and show the accuracy of warnings about vintage negatives.

### Chosen Test Negatives

I sorted through negatives from a variety of different decades, selecting candidates from different eras. I labeled them with a date and the negative format (size). I also grouped them into what I believed were nitrate and non-nitrate batches. Since none of the negatives exhibited advanced deterioration attributable to specific types of negatives, the negative date was the primary 'guess' as to whether the negative was nitrate or acetate. However, an additional notation was made for those that exhibited a strong vinegar smell that is typical of acetate negatives.

## Nitrate Burn Tests

The negatives deemed nitrate were tested first, with a log kept of each burn test, noting the negative date and size.

### Videos: www.phototree.com/burn.htm

---

Note: Still photographs are used in this book to illustrate the burn tests, however videos of the complete tests can be viewed at www.phototree.com/burn.htm. These videos are surprising and enlightening.

---

### Nitrate Burn Results

Nitrate negatives immediately ignited when a flame touched an edge and within two seconds rapidly accelerated to a flash-fire state. One of the characteristics of nitrate material is that its molecules contain chemically combined oxygen that is released when heated; essentially creating its own oxygen that continuously feeds the fire until the fuel (negative) is depleted.[5]

Nitrate film can become a flash fire in seconds.

The nitrate fire will engulf and burn the entire negative in just a few seconds. You can see how it could ignite adjacent negatives and other materials easily, especially since nitrate film burns hotter than gasoline.7

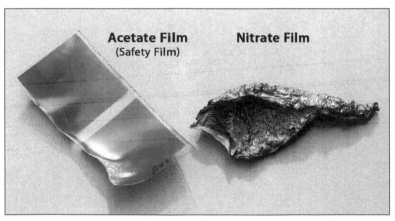

Nitrate film becomes crumbling ash, acetate film harmlessly melts.

## Acetate and Polyester Burn Tests

Burn tests on acetate and polyester film were conducted in the same manner as tests on nitrate films.

---

Tip – Acetate and polyester negatives are NOT a fire hazard.

---

Acetate film, also called Safety Film, was developed in response to the danger that nitrate film posed. Safety film resists burning; it simply melts and curls under direct flame. Polyester film, the most modern film technology exhibits similar characteristics when exposed to fire.

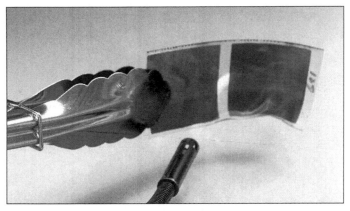

Flame placed on Safety Film edge; it only melts and curls.

The videos of Safety Film show its stubbornness and resistance to flames. The negatives simply curl and melt.

## Summary of Hazards

The detailed explanation of nitrate and acetate film characteristics and hazards should be read with carefully if you have vintage negatives. Correct storage is important to eliminating environments that promote deterioration; the next chapter covers this in detail.

## Important Steps for Reducing Hazards

- Determine the probability of nitrate film by sorting film by age:
    - Pre-1950 film may be nitrate.
- Check film for physical deterioration listed in this chapter.
- Isolate and store nitrate films as describe in the next chapter.
- Remove film with advanced deterioration.

# More Resources

The National Park Service has developed a comprehensive guide for museum management titled NPS Museum Handbook. This guide includes Appendix (M), titled *Management of Cellulose Nitrate and Cellulose Ester Film*

If you wish to explore the subject of hazardous films, this is one of the most complete works available. It can be found on the NPS website:

http://www.nps.gov/history/museum/publications/handbook.html

## Additional Sources of Information

In addition, there are many comprehensive scientific and professional papers available on the subject. Here are a few from respected institutions.

Kodak - Storage and Handling of Processed Nitrate Film
http://motion.kodak.com/motion/Support/Technical_Information/Storage/storage_nitrate.htm

Northeast Document Conversation Center
http://www.nedcc.org/assets/media/documents/05PH_01FilmBaseGuide.pdf

AMIA – Identifying and Handling Nitrate Film
http://www.amianet.org/groups/committees/nitrate/documents/NitrateIGNov08.pdf

HSE (UK) – The Dangers of Cellulous Nitrate Film
http://www.hse.gov.uk/pubns/indg469.pdf

National Park Service – Identification of Photographic Materials
http://www.nps.gov/museum/publications/conserveogram/14-09.pdf

National Park Service – Disposal of Cellulose Nitrate Film
http://www.nps.gov/museum/publications/conserveogram/02-22.pdf

# CARE, STORAGE, & PRESERVATION

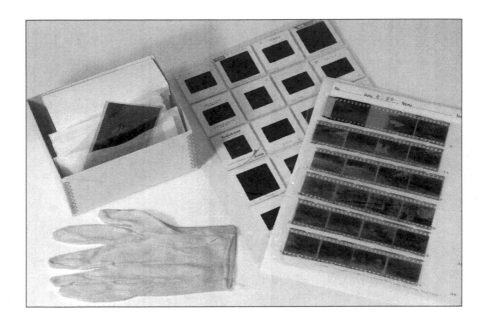

Storage conditions recommended for photographic prints also apply to negatives and slides. Extreme temperatures and humidity may result in damage to the film, and prolonged exposure to sunlight should be avoided.

Negatives and slides are easy to protect and archive, providing a source for new prints for a very long time. Two levels of storage are involved; one is protecting the individual piece of film in a sleeve or archival envelope, the second is storing the sleeves themselves.

Negative and slide pages are available for any size and format.

## Handling Negatives

Fingerprints will be more visible on film than on paper prints. The fingerprints cannot be removed easily and they reduce film clarity, affecting quality of future prints you wish to create.

### By the Edges

Hold a negative or slide by the film's edges. The safest manner for handling film is to wear special, but economical, gloves designed for such use.

### Photographer Gloves

Soft, thin white cotton gloves are used by professionals and hobbyists when handling film. When handling or sorting a large number of negatives or slides, it is advisable to take the extra time to don gloves.

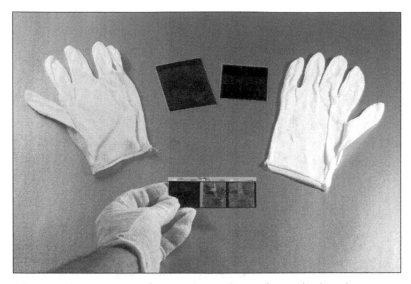

Cotton gloves prevent fingerprints, oil transfer, and other damage.

Inexpensive gloves are available from a variety of sources including these gloves are from Amazon.com.

## Protective Sleeves

A wide variety of archival-safe plastic sleeves are available to protect film. These are highly recommended for archival piece of mind, and convenience if you wish to access the negatives frequently.

Tip – Check film for excess dust or dirt before inserting film into sleeves. Clean the film if necessary before inserting, as inserting dirty film may deposit the dirt inside the sleeve, contaminating the film every time it is re-inserted.

### Negatives

Negatives were seldom touched after prints were returned to consumer photographers. They usually spent their life in the accompanying print envelope. This is good however, as they were never handled and harmed.

A convenient method of archiving negatives is inserting them into full-page sleeves that fit into 3-ring binders. Different format pages accommodate the variety of negative sizes. The PrintFile (www.printfile.com) brand of archival sleeves are archival save and conform to the Photographic Activity Test (PAT) standards. We use them almost exclusively because they are a trusted product and are easily found online and in camera stores. Sleeves are available for most negatives sizes.

## 35mm Negatives

These pages come in several widths, accommodating film strips of 4, 5, or 6 negatives. We like the 5-width pages as we have seldom seen 6-width negative strips, and the wider pages do not fit well in a standard 3-ring binder.

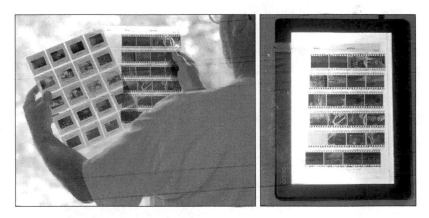

When placed in full page sleeves, negatives (and slides) are easy to preview by holding up to a light, or placed on a light table.

## 120 and 127 Format Negatives

The 120 negatives are typically 2¼" x 2¼" or 2¼" x 3¼, and are frequently found throughout the 20th century. They are commonly called medium format and are still used by professional photographers. The 120 format negative sleeves accommodate 127 negatives also, as the 127 negatives are narrower at 1 5/8" wide but fit nicely into the same 120 sleeves.

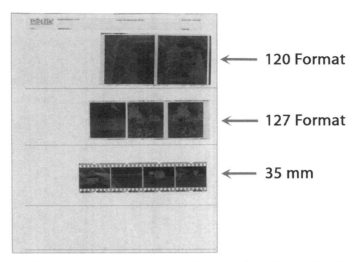

120 Format pages can accommodate a variety of negative sizes.

## APS Format Negatives

Nearly all the camera and film manufacturers in the early 1990s agreed on a new film format that was supposed to spur sales by enabling smaller and easier to operate cameras, with new features such as the ability to take panorama photographs. In 1996, the APS (Advanced Photo System) was introduced at a major photographic trade show in Las Vegas.

Advantix was the Kodak brand for APS film.

The most noticeable characteristic of the new standard was a self-loading, auto-rewinding film. It was slightly smaller than standard 35mm film, and allowed APS-enabled cameras to take pictures in one of three formats or aspect ratios: 1) High definition, 2) classic mode, 3) panorama.

APS film production ceased in 2011; the new system failed to gain commercial success due to ridicule by professional and advanced photographers, lower quality images than 35mm film, and the advancing popularity of digital cameras.

However, during its short life, millions of negatives were created by photographers who did purchase and use the new APS standard.

For digital archiving and reproduction purposes, the APS system presents a unique challenge to the owner of these negatives. When the film was developed and prints created, the film was rewound into the canister for eternal storage. A lab or photo printing service needed special machines to pull out the negative and print photographs. These capabilities are quickly disappearing, as the film format has been obsolete for over 10 years.

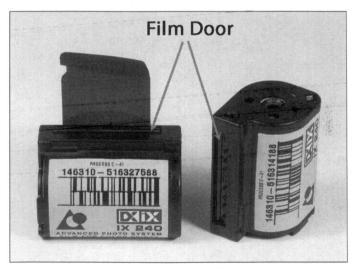

APS film was secure behind a spring-loaded cartridge door.

I suggest you remove the developed negatives from APS cartridges and store them in the same manner as other negatives: in protective sleeves. To accomplish this, a few steps are required to remove the negatives from the cartridge. This task does require a small screwdriver to open the film door and un-wind the film so it protrudes from the cartridge.

The first step is to swing the little door open so the negative can exit the cartridge. This is accomplished by inserting a small screwdriver or similar object into a round slot on either end of the cartridge, and twisting it to open the door. The door does not always stay open; keep it open with a fingernail or other small object.

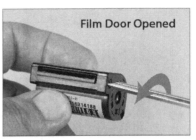

Cartridge door can be opened by twisting a round slot.

Using the same small flathead screwdriver, insert it into the center hole of the cartridge and turn it in a direction that will unwind the film; this can be done on either end.

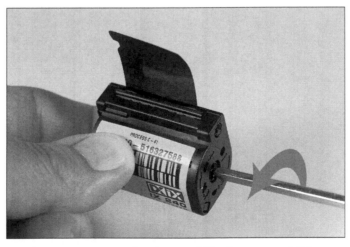

Rotate center mechanism until film becomes visible.

The film should peek out the door, at which time the door will stay open and you can gently pull the film out of the canister.

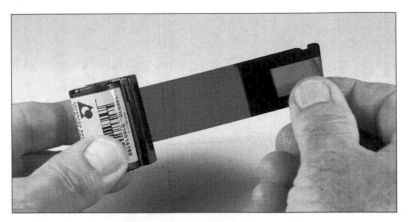

Slowly pull negative out of the cartridge.

Tip – The film will have a profound curl. With the cartridge still attached, hang the film by attaching some masking tape or similar to the free end and tape to a doorframe, mantle, or some other place so the film can hang freely; weighted by the empty cartridge. Nearly all the curl will disappear within a few hours.

Once the film is fully extended from the cartridge, it still will not come loose from the cartridge as the design was intended to facilitate rewinding back into the cartridge. Cut the film from the cartridge with scissors, there is plenty of trailer stock on the film to cut clear of the last image.

Cut the long roll of negatives into film strips that fit into standard 35mm sleeve pages; usually five to six images per strip. The chapter on scanning will explain how to scan these odd-sized negatives.

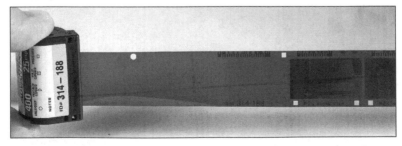

Cut negative from cartridge, leaving one inch trailer next to last frame.

## Larger Negatives: 116 and 122 (Postcard) Formats

116 format negatives were introduced in 1899 and were still very popular in the 1930s and 40s. Prints were made the same size as the negative; these are commonly called contact prints. Many photographs from these negatives are found in vintage black-page albums, while the negatives are usually housed in their original envelopes. Pages designed for 4" x 5" negatives are best for 116 format film.

4" x 5" Negative pages are perfect for 116 format negatives.

Many older collections include postcard size negatives, which were even larger (3¼" by 5½); these fit best in sleeves designed for 5" x 7" prints.

116 and 122 Format (postcard) negatives.

Appendix A lists over 30 different film sizes. Larger negative sleeves such as those for 4" x 5" negatives will accommodate most oversized formats. The largest negative such as 8" x 10" will require a full-page sleeve. Here are some sample PrintFile negative pages.

## PrintFile Brand Negative Sleeves

- 35-7B Negative Pages – Holds seven 35mm strips of five frames.
- 120-3HB Negative Pages – Holds four 120 or 127 strips of three frames.
- 45-4B Negative Pages – Holds four, 4" x 5" or smaller negatives.

# Glassine Paper Envelopes

Archival paper envelopes are also available for negatives. These are typically used for nitrate and larger negatives, though 35mm paper holders are also available. Negatives placed in paper envelopes, are usually then stored in archival boxes.

This type of storage is popular with professional photographers and museums, since it is does not require 3-ring binders, and boxes of envelopes store more efficiently. Another advantage of paper sleeves is that information about the negative can be written on the envelope.

Glassine envelopes are the preferred archival paper envelope. They are made from a smooth paper (will not scratch negatives), are acid-free, and water-resistant. They are not waterproof, but can repel inadvertent splashes. Glassine envelopes are translucent, allowing you to recognize the image when held up to light or placed on a light table.

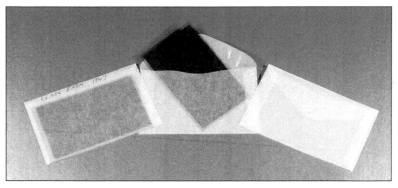

Place only one negative or negative strip in each glassine envelope.

Glassine envelopes are available from most archive and photography stores including through internet websites. They fit easily in small acid-free photo boxes.

## Storing Glassine Envelopes

Glassine envelopes were designed to breath, that is let any build-up of gases and moisture escape from the negative. This is especially important for older negatives that tend to break down over time. Newer negatives do not have the problem of chemical breakdown, so plastic sleeves are suitable, though newer film can be stored in proper paper envelopes or sleeves.

Glassine envelopes are best stored in archival boxes.

To facilitate the breathing, you do not want to store the paper sleeves in plastic sheets or in sealed boxes, this would defeat the purpose. Glassine envelopes should be stored in acid-free archival boxes made of dense paper material or cardboard. These archival boxes are available from a variety of sources, including large online stores.

## Mounted Slides

35mm slides from the 1950s through the 1990s are included in most family photograph collections. This author sat through many travelogue presentations by my father to polite audiences of relatives and friends.

Early Kodachrome slide film produced outstanding color and clarity, and improved slide film is still used today to make museum quality prints.

Color 35mm slides are the most common, though monochrome (black and white) slides are occasionally found and medium format ( 2¼" x 2¼") color slides were available.

127 Format Color Slide

35mm BW Slide

35mm Color Slide

120 Format Color Slide

Slide transparencies were available in a variety of formats.

## Original Slide Box Storage

Slides were usually returned from the film developer in small boxes; the boxes came in many sizes and shapes, some were even plastic.

Original slide boxes and trays protect the slides.

There is nothing wrong in storing slides in their original boxes or trays; it is just not easy to review them. If you do keep them in the boxes and trays, save your sanity and identify the subject matter on the outside of the box, including slide topics and approximate date. Luckily, many slide mounts were printed with the development date. In addition, most tray boxes included a log area where you could record information on individual slides.

I rejoice when I find old trays with descriptions that someone took the time to identify each slide.

## Carousels and Trays

The first iconic Kodak Carousel projector was introduced in 1961.[7] This technological marvel represents Americana as much as any commercial product. The Carousel and other types of slide projectors were a popular if not a boring part of every vacation review. The corporate world latched onto the presentation method with vigor, using it for meetings and sales pitches. While the underlying technology has changed, the ubiquitous Microsoft PowerPoint program uses the term slide as the description of each page in a presentation.

Many of us have hundreds of slides in plastic trays for which we no longer have a projector. It does not hurt the slides to live in the cartridges. They are protected from general physical damage. However, to review them without a projector, you must take each one out, and hold it up to a light source. Using this method of review, you may transfer fingerprints, dirt, and oil to the slide while handling it. I recommend you move the slides to convenient sheets of plastic sleeves.

## Archival Slide Pages

A full archival slide page designed for 35mm slides accommodates 20 slides, four per row with five rows on a single page. They store nicely in a 3-ring binder for easy access.

Full-page sleeve with individual pockets for slides.

These pages are easy to review and they protect your slides. In addition, the page can be labeled with a marker identifying the subject matter. They can be found in most camera stores, online archival websites, and Amazon.com.

## Binders and Boxes

Once your slides and negatives are safely placed in protective pages, you need to organize and store the pages. Of course, the full sheet sleeves were designed for placement into 3-ring binders; but which binder?

The shortest answer is to use PVC-free binders that are easily available at office and discount stores. Most current binders found today are PVC free. This includes the most commonly found Avery, ClearVue, and Wilson Jones brand binders. Generic economy binders may not be PVC free and should be avoided.

## Archive Safe 3-Ring Binders

We all have 3-ring binders storing various documents. There is generally no way to tell if older binders are PVC-free, so you may want to refresh your collection for safe archiving.

I find it helps film management if you use the type of binder that has a spine label holder that allows you to insert a description of the contents; just as appears on the spine of a book. A view pocket on the front is useful also for labeling the binder. If you have many binders, the visual clue as to the contents makes research a lot smoother.

Archival box binder and three-ring binders with identification

## Archival Boxes with Rings

A professional way of storing your protective pages, and other documents, is with binder boxes. These archival boxes have 3-ring mechanisms built into the box. I find these a little awkward for frequent use, but they are great for long-term storing of valuable negatives, slides, and documents.

They are considerably more expensive than standard three-ring binders are, yet these models do offer extra levels of protection since they close like a box.

Archival box with 3-ring mechanism.

## Professional Binders

Library and museum grade binders are very nice, yet quite expensive. These binders have hinged covers, are very durable, and hardboard front and back. The ring mechanism is usually more durable than retail binders and will not let sleeves or documents slip out of the rings. Bindertek has a nice selection of these at premium prices, though the binders will last for a considerable time.

Archival binders typically used by libraries and museums.

## Archival Product Sources

Binders are available at office supply and discount stores. Greater selections can be found online and with specialty suppliers such as these:

| | |
|---|---|
| Amazon.com | Variety of archival products |
| Archival Methods | Full catalog of archival products |
| Bindertek | Binders and accessories |
| Gaylord | Full catalog of archival products |
| Hollinger | Binders and boxes |
| PrintFile | Protective sleeves and binders |

## Acid-Free Archival Products

Acid-free binders are usually made of polypropylene that is widely used in archival products. PVC based products are not recommended for archival applications as they can deteriorate and emit acidic fumes.

Nearly all binder companies explicitly list 'PVC-Free' in their product descriptions. Recent examination of Avery brand binders in stores revealed the claim on each binder. Trusted brands realize this is a requirement for archival applications and have adjusted their product manufacturing accordingly. This is also true for plastic (polypropylene) sleeves designed for film and slides.

Appendix B includes detailed specifications and definitions of archival standards.

## Light Box for Easy Viewing

Light boxes are frames or boxes covered with frosted glass or translucent plastic that is backlit by a light source. These have been used for decades to view slides and negatives by professional and amateur photographers. These handy devices take much of the tedium out of viewing slides and negatives.

The 8" x 10" Gepe Illuminator Kit is a convenient and useful size.

New uses for light boxes have caused the name to change to a more modern description, though not necessarily a clearer term. You will find them with descriptions such as:

- Light box
- Light tray
- Light pad
- Light tracing pad
- Illuminator kit

These devices are also used for tracing designs, scrapbooking, and even as a background for photographing small objects. All versions work fine for viewing negatives and slides.

Light boxes and their similar named cousins, can be found at most on-line photography sources and Amazon.com. I purchased my 8"x10" Gepe Illuminator Kit from B&Hphoto.com, and find this size is ideal for easy storage.

# CLEANING SLIDES AND NEGATIVES

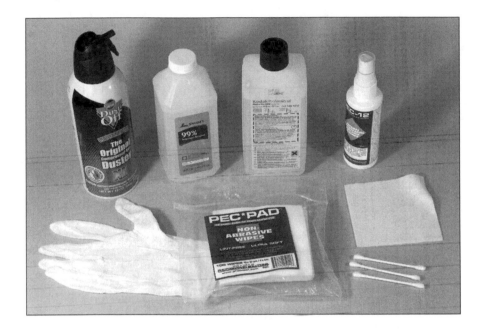

$M$ost negatives and slides do not need extensive cleaning as they have been stored in envelopes, boxes, trays, or possibly plastic sleeves most of their life. However, many will have collected dust even from minimal handling.

## Dust Removal

Dust is a particular concern with negatives and slides since the film must be scanned at very high resolution to produce a good image; dust particles will appear as white spots or even strings.

There are several methods of removing dust, and the combination of them will produce the best and safest results. The three methods incorporate:

- Canned (compressed) air
- Camel hair brushes
- Anti-static photo cloths

### Canned Air

A vigorous blast of canned air to both sides of the slide or negative will eliminate much of the dust, especially large loose pieces.

---

Tip – When using compressed air, hold the can upright, not angled or pointed down; this will reduce moisture from being expelled. I always direct the first puff of air at my hand to see if it is mostly moisture.

---

Hold the film or negative at an angle to the air stream so the dust can blow away. Directing the spray directly at the flat surface may just scatter the dust, leaving some on the film. Clean both sides of the film.

### Soft Brush

The commonly named camel-hair brush is a generic term for soft brushes, yet it actually has no camel hair in it, as camel hair is too coarse for use on delicate surfaces. Urban legend states that a man named Mr. Camel invented the use of soft animal hair for brushes, and his name stuck to nearly all animal hair brushes.

Use a soft brush designed for film cleaning from a trusted source.

Camel-hair brushes can be made of a variety of animal hair and synthetic materials, with a range of softness. Beware of generic brushes from general stores. If you want a brush for cleaning negatives or slides, purchase one from a trusted photography source such as B&Hphoto or Adorama.

If a negative or slide is exceptionally dusty or dirty, use a blast of canned air first to remove the larger pieces. This will help prevent scratching the surface by moving large pieces with the brush.

Swipe the brush gently in one direction on the negative or slide, remembering to clean both sides. When finished cleaning film, shake or flick the brush to remove accumulated dust. Most dust on the film was from the air around it. If the brush is left out or stored in an area frequently accessed, it also will accumulate dust. Store it in a closed container or small storage bag.

## Anti-Static Cleaning Cloth

PEC-Pads are soft, lint-free cotton cloths designed for cleaning film, camera lenses, and other delicate surfaces. These are available in 100-packs at Amazon and B&H Photo. These also can be used to clean your scanner glass, computer and mobile devices screens, and eyeglasses.

PEC-Pad lint-free cleaning cloths.

## Stains, Mold, Fungus, Unexplained Gunk

Negatives and slides that have been subjected to floods, poor storage conditions, and rough handling may surface contamination that goes beyond mere dust. Water stains, molds, and other material are not easily removed by simply brushing or blowing air across the film. Not unlike dirt on your kitchen surface, some negatives and slides will require application of a cleaning agent.

A variety of cleaners for removing stubborn stains on negatives and slides are available; the differences between them are the cleaning agents in the solution.

Three different methods or solutions were used to clean negatives and slides for illustration. These include:

- Wiping with 98% alcohol
- Wiping with PEC (Photographic Emulsion Cleaner)
- Soaking in Kodak Photo-Flo

All products have been satisfactorily tested by PhotoTree.com.

Cleaners for all needs: Photo-Flo 200, 99% Alcohol, Pec-12 Cleaner

Tip – Remember to blow the negative or slide with compressed air to remove loose dust and dirt before attempting cleaning.

## Alcohol Wipe – Kodak Recommended

The Kodak website offers a wide range of technical information regarding many aspects of handling, cleaning, and storage of negatives and slides. Many of their recommendations are summarized here, and links to the original article are included.

Throughout the published technical information, Kodak consistently recommends using 98% isopropyl alcohol for cleaning negatives and slides.

This strength of alcohol is not widely available. Drugstore and discount stores typically carry 70% alcohol; the other 30% is water. The diluted alcohols will not evaporate as quickly and will leave streaks or water strains. Higher strength (98% or 99%) alcohol can be found at Amazon.com and local medical supply stores.

## Alcohol cleaning steps for 35 mm negatives:

- Wear a cotton glove on the hand that will hold the negative.
- Wet a PEC-Pad with alcohol to moisten, do not saturate.
- Fold the pad in half, grip the negative gently, and slide the negative through the folded pad to clean the negative.
- If needed, wipe a couple times, using a clean pad area or use another pad. Each wipe should be with a clean of the pad.
- If alcohol streaks remain, wipe with a dry pad.

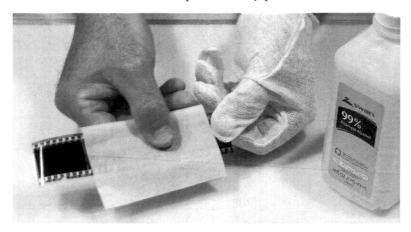

Cleaning 35mm film with alcohol and a PEC-Pad.

If the image to be cleaned is a 35mm slide, Kodak recommends taking it out of the plastic or cardboard frame. This may not be desired if you do not have replacement frames. Careful use of an alcohol dampened pad may work fine on a framed slide, though you may not be able to clean to the edges of the slide film.

## Alcohol cleaning steps for framed slide:

- Hold the slide firmly on a clean, dry surface with one hand.
- Moisten a small section of a PEC-Pad.
- Gently wipe the slide clean.
- When dry, turn slide over and repeat action.

Large format negatives require a little more manual handling, but can be cleaned just the same.

## Alcohol cleaning steps for a large format negative:

- Place negative on a clean, dry surface, PEC-Pad is good.
- Moisten a large portion of a PEC-Pad with alcohol.
- Wrap pad around index finger and wipe negative.
- Reposition pad to a clean area to wipe untouched area.
- When negative is dry, turn over onto a clean area and repeat.
- Inspect negative and repeat as necessary.

Large format negative placed on a PEC-Pad for cleaning.

Tip – Do not wipe negative with a used portion of the pad. Always begin each wipe with a clean pad or pad area.

# PEC-12 – Photographic Emulsion Cleaner

PEC-12 is a waterless Photographic Emulsion Cleaner that is suitable for use on most film and print emulsions.[8]

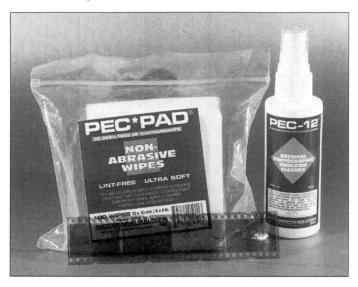

PEC-12 Cleaner and PEC-Pads.

It is designed to remove stains such as grease pencil, adhesive residue, finger oils, ball-point pen, fungus, smoke & soot damage. It will not remove water based stains; the next section on soaking in Photo-Flo will address those problems.

PEC-12 is safe to use on color negatives, black and white negatives, and slides. However, it is recommended that you test your cleaning technique on an unimportant piece of film first. Read the comprehensive recommendations on the PEC website if desired.

### PEC-12 cleaning steps for 35mm negatives:

- Wear cotton glove on the hand that will hold the negative.
- Moisten a PEC-Pad with PEC-12, do not oversaturate.
- Fold the pad in half, grip the negative gently, and slide the negative through the folded pad to clean the negative.

- If needed, wipe a couple of times, either moving the pad to a clean area or using another pad. Use a clean pad area for each wipe.
- The cleaner should evaporate immediately.
- If too much cleaner was used, a film may be left behind. Wipe again with only a slightly moistened pad.

---

Tip – If only a small area on negative needs cleaning, a cotton swab moistened with PEC-12 can be used.

---

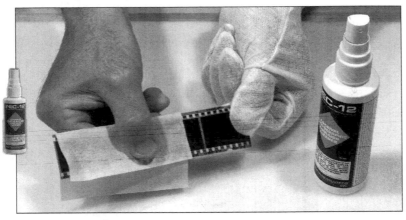

Moisten pad slightly with PEC-12, do not spray on negative.

If the image to be cleaned is a 35mm slide, it may be easier to clean the slide with a cotton swab rather than a PE-Pad. This may be desired if you do not have replacement frames.

## PEC-12 cleaning steps for framed slides:

- Hold the slide firmly on a clean, dry surface with one hand.
- Spray a small section of a PEC-Pad or cotton swab.
- Gently wipe the slide clean with single strokes.
- When dry, turn slide over and repeat action.

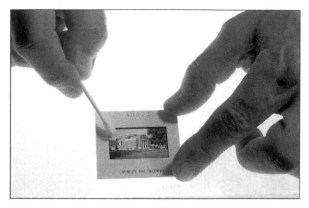

Cleaning a mounted slide with a cotton swab.

---

Tip – When using a cotton swab, do not wipe with a back and forth motion, you may smear the material you are trying to remove. Use single strokes from one side to the other, rotating the swab to a clean place each stroke. If required, use multiple swabs.

---

Check closely to see if the swab left behind small cotton strands; remove any strands with air, a brush, or a PEC-Pad.

### PEC-12 cleaning steps for a large format negative:

- Place negative on a clean, dry surface, PEC-Pad is good.
- Hold in place with a gloved hand.
- Moisten a large portion of the PEC-Pad with PEC-12.
- Wrap pad around index finger and wipe negative.
- Reposition pad to a clean area to wipe untouched area.
- When negative is dry, turn over onto a clean area and repeat.
- Inspect negative and repeat as necessary.

## Re-Wash Negatives

Another treatment for removing heavy dust, major water stains, or separating negatives stuck together is to soak them in a liquid bath. This bath is mostly distilled water and a photographic surfactant or water softener.

Kodak Photo-Flo and distilled water for tough water stains.

Photo-Flo 200 is a Kodak product used in the final rinse of film developing. A small amount is added to distilled water; reducing streaking, water spots, and improving drying time. Photo-Flo 200 can be found in photography supply stores and from Amazon.com.

The product is specifically used during the final rinse of black and white film development, but is also useful for re-washing color films.

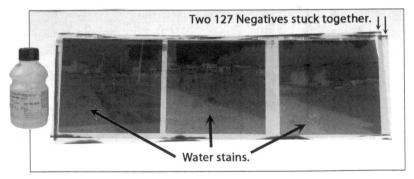

Two 127 Negatives stuck together.

Water stains.

Kodak Photo-Flo soaking solution.

Note: It is important to follow product directions when adding Photo-Flo to the distilled water. A very small amount is only required. Excess will not cause damage, but will make the solution too thick and frothy, and may leave streaks.

**PHOTO-FLO cleaning steps:**

- Clean negatives with compressed air first.
- Wipe with isopropyl alcohol for extremely dirty negatives.
- Mix Photo-Flo & distilled water as per instructions.
- Place negative(s) in solution for one to two minutes.
- Grasp the negative end, and vigorously agitate, causing solution to flow over negative.
- Remove from solution and hang to drip-dry.
- Hang from a clip or run a string through a perforation for 35mm film and hang for drying.
- Immediately after drying, place in clean sleeve or scan (with clean scanner glass), then place in clean sleeve.

---

Tip – Negatives will nearly always pick up dust in the average household. Blow clean with compressed air before each scanning. Dust nearly always shows up as white specks or strings.

---

## Separating Negatives Stuck Together

Negatives are sometimes found stuck together. This most likely happens when 35mm negatives are stored in their original paper folders. They may have been exposed to moisture or high humidity, and mold may have grown between them.

DO NOT attempt to pull them apart; the emulsion on one or both negatives might peel off the base material.

Soak them in the described Photo-Flo solution for several minutes; they may separate on their own. (We have soaked both black and white and color negatives up to 30 minutes with no damage).

If they do not separate on their own, gently pull one end apart, while the negatives are still in the solution. Place a soft object like a cotton swab between the strips, creating very light tension, and continue soaking. Repeat until negatives separate.

Hang negatives from a clip to air dry.

Once the negatives have been washed, shake excess solution from them and hang to air dry. A common bag clip or binder clip attached to an end of the negative works well. The Photo-Flo solution allows the water to drain evenly from the negative, while not leaving water spots. The negative should dry within two hours in a normal household environment so you can scan them.

These negatives may require further cleaning. Let them thoroughly dry at least 24 hours, as the emulsion may have become soft and you may scratch or smudge it using one of the previously described cleaning processes.

This process can also be used to salvage negatives coated with gunk or stained from a flood. Kodak provides excellent guidance on their web page titled *Flood Damaged Photographs* (http://www.kodak.com/global/en/service/faqs/faq0700.shtml)

# COMMERCIAL SCANNING SERVICES

$A$s noted in the introduction, negatives can provide us with some of the best images from the past since many negatives are in perfect condition. Negatives are like backups of prints that you may have lost, given away, or were damaged. You may discover negatives of prints you never knew existed. I have found this has been especially exciting when looking at negatives from 50 to 90 years ago – yes, I am lucky to have so many from my ancestors.

However, to enjoy the negatives you need to have prints made from them – or at least have viewable images created. Today, this is easy, much easier than taking the negatives in for reprints. By digitally scanning them, you can not only have prints made, but also can share the images via a variety of avenues such as email, blogs, and social media.

Scanning hundreds of negatives is a tedious task.

Negative scanning can be lengthy and tedious. One of the decisions many family archivists have to decide is whether to scan the negatives themselves or have them scanned by a professional service. Both options, along with their advantages and disadvantages are discussed here.

## Commercial Scanning Services

Many companies offer scanning services for negatives and slides; some in your local community and many accessible over the internet. If possible, I like to use a local service as it eliminates the need and cost of shipping, and the turn-around time is usually shorter. In addition, you have a person to talk to about your project.

Some scanning services offer a variety of scan resolutions (DPI), each with a different price. The family archivist many not understand the need and use of each. For most non-commercial uses, the expensive, highest resolution scan is not needed.

## Local Services - Professional

You may find some local, established photo processing companies in your area; they are called labs in the photography business, as all film before digital technology was developed in a laboratory (darkroom). Simply search the internet for "photo lab [your city]", and local companies should be returned by your search engine.

These local full-service labs will provide the best results, however they probably will be the most expensive. They primarily cater to the professional photographer or design agency, and their offerings are not as price-sensitive as consumer services. One advantage labs usually offer is the ability to scan unique negatives such as 5x7 sizes that national chain stores cannot.

## Local Services – Consumer

You may have several options available for inexpensive yet acceptable scans from local stores of national companies. The large discount stores, including membership chains, usually have photo labs in the store, or have quick access to a central lab. They can usually scan slides and negatives at a medium resolution for an acceptable price.

While I have several scanners, I have used Costco, one of the warehouse retailers, for years to scan hundreds of 35mm slides my father took of vacations, reunions, and other events. The scanned slide images were written on a DVD as JPG files, which are easy to view. These images are 2400 DPI, suitable for most casual uses. If there is a particular image that I want enlarged or if I am interested in a small area of the image, I then scan it on one of my scanners at a higher resolution.

Scanning services save your images to convenient CDs or DVDs.

For about 25 cents per image, the price of scanning a large quantity of slides and negatives is well worth the cost. The large stores usually send negatives or slides to a central processing lab, and the order may take a few days.

---

Note: Some experts do not consider the inexpensive, bulk processing 'archival quality'. This may be true for museums, libraries, official archives, professional archivists, and others. However, for the family historian, low-cost bulk commercial scans will serve desired goals, and provide an easy and inexpensive means to a family's archival requirements.

---

## Size, Formats, and Use

As scanner technology changes, service companies need to upgrade or replace their equipment just like consumers. Some scanning services provide 2400 and 4800 DPI scanning. The current resolutions listed on numerous popular online services in 2014 list available resolutions as 2000, 3000, and 4000 DPI.

Just like Goldilocks' preference in porridge and beds, I prefer the middle version of scan resolution for most applications. The lowest resolutions do not provide enough detail; the highest resolutions are too expensive for family archives.

When I scan my own negatives and slides, I scan at 2400 DPI for most images. This is a nice size for detail, yet produces a small file size and scans in an acceptable time.

## Scanning Resolution and Costs – 35mm

The following table provides a guideline for costs and appropriate use for the listed resolutions. Actual cost can vary widely; shop around, yet try to find an established, reputable company.

| Resolution (DPI | Sample Cost ($) | Use or Application |
|---|---|---|
| 2400 - 3000 | .29 - .78 | Up to 8 x 10 prints, Email, Web pages Social Media, Archive |
| 4000 | 38.1.20 | Up to 12 x 18 prints, Photo Trestoration, Professional Archive |

Note: The above table applies to 35mm slides and negatives. Larger film will cost more.

## Large Size Negatives

Many companies do not list scanning options for large negatives such as the 120, 127, and 116 formats. Ask your local scanning companies about large negatives and search for internet services that offer an economical plan.

## Advantages of Scanning Services

- Great source if you do not have scanning capabilities.
- Tedium of scanning eliminated.
- Good quality files returned.
- Conveniently loaded onto a DVD or CD.

## Disadvantages of Scanning Services

- Turnaround time can be weeks for remote services.
- Up-charges for high resolution or quick scan time.
- Some services only offer a minimum price package.
- Shipping costs incurred to and from remote service.
- Communications with company not always smooth.
- Prices vary greatly

# NEGATIVE SCANNING - PERSONAL

Consumer scanning has become dramatically easier and more economical in the last ten years. During this time, flatbed scanners have dropped in price from more than $1,000.00 to under $200.00 for excellent scanner quality and advanced features.

## Choosing a Scanner

Which scanner is best for your projects? This is similar to asking which automobile is best. The multitude of brands and models excel at different tasks; and cost is always a consideration. This book is primarily for the consumer and addresses their needs to preserve and copy slides and negatives for family history, genealogy, and general archiving.

## Types of Film Scanners

The term 'film' will apply to both negatives and slides when discussing generic topics. Negatives and slides are both film.

Film scanners come in three classes:

- Dedicated, expensive film scanners, for professional use.
- Small one-touch film scanners, including portable devices.
- Flatbed scanner with special features for film scanning.

**Dedicated film scanners** provide the highest quality results and are used by professional scanning services. These can be very expensive, and are overkill for the average consumer archivist. These are not reviewed in this book, but can be found from such respectable companies such as Nikon, Minolta, and others.

High-End scanners are overkill for most consumer tasks.

**Small inexpensive scanners,** while cute and simple, will not provide the quality desired from most films. The resolution is usually low and not adjustable, and the scanner cannot accept a range of film sizes. This would prevent you from making high-quality enlargements from a scan or enlarging a portion of the film to focus on a single person. These look attractive due to their small cost, but none are recommended for archival quality scanning.

Inexpensive scanners offer few options for the home archivist.

**Flatbed scanners** come in many forms, with different features, capabilities, and prices, yet the choices narrow considerably when negative and slide-scanning requirements are factored in. The most useful scanners for the tasks outlined in this book, include:

- The ability to scan different size  negatives.
- Can scan slides (positive transparencies).
- Saves images at high resolutions and in a variety of formats.

These requirements usually eliminate the following types of scanners from consideration for archival scanning:

- Auto-feed scanners.
- Hand-held or portable scanners.
- All-in-one scanners.

Scanners that meet the archivist's requirements are readily available at office supply stores, electronics stores, and online. Advancements in technology have also reduced costs of these scanners greatly; high quality, full-featured scanners can be purchased for under $200.00.

Canon 9000F (l) and Epson V500 (r) both include negative & slide capabilities.

I currently use two flatbed scanners for various projects: An Epson V500 and a Canon 9000F. I have written reviews on both of these, including scan-time tests that are posted on PhotoTree.com. Both scanners produce great results, though the Canon model has shorter scan times that may be important if you are scanning a large number of negatives or slides.

Epson and Canon scanners (and their successors) are readily available from many sources. Each scanner company has numerous models; some less, some more expensive than the ones mentioned here. Your scanner of choice should have capabilities and templates to handle various size films.

## Scanner Software

Scanners come with software that allows you control the device and allow you to change settings to fit your needs. Install the software following instructions included with the scanner. Most scanners include buttons that perform one-touch scanning. However, many times the settings associated with this button may not produce the scan you want or need. Become familiar with the software and use it to create the images suitable for archiving.

## Understanding Compression & File Formats

While they are not explicitly dependent on each other, file compression and file formats are closely connected.

### JPG versus TIF Files

There are long-running narratives about JPG vs. TIF formats; as to which one is better or recommended. It depends on what your goal is or desired use of the file. To be clear, there are many image file formats for use with photographs, however JPG and TIF are the most common and dependable formats. First, a short definition of each will introduce the two most common file types to you.

**TIF** – The TIF (Tagged Image File) is a Lossless file format, meaning it maintains all original detail in the image. It is recommended for archival quality images, and is likely to be a readable standard far into the future. The disadvantage of TIF files is their size, they can become quite large. (Note: The format is also known as TIFF, Tagged Image File Format.)

**JPG** – The JPG (Joint Photographic Group) format is a Lossy file format, meaning it uses a compression formula that reduces the file size, but it also loses some detail during compression. This format does allow the compression amount to be adjusted, with greater compression losing more detail, and less compression preserving more detail. (Note: This format is also called JPEG.)

The following table summarizes the characteristics of TIF and JPG files.

| File Format | Compression Technique | Loses Detail | Variable Compression | File Size |
|---|---|---|---|---|
| TIF | Lossless | No | No | Large |
| JPG | Lossly | Yes | Yes | Small to Medium |

## Additional File Formats

Numerous other file formats are available to store digital images, each with their advantages or disadvantages, and each with their supporters and detractors. The following is a complete list of file formats recognized and recommended by the Library of Congress.[9]

- TIFF (uncompressed)
- JPEG2000 (lossless) (*.jp2)
- PNG (*.png)
- JPEG/JFIF (*.jpg)
- Digital Negative DNG (*.dng)
- JPEG2000 (lossy) (*.jp2)
- TIFF (compressed)
- BMP (*.bmp)
- GIF (*.gif)

Most scanners do not create all the above formats. Generally, they can create TIF (TIFF) and JPG. These two formats will support any need of the family archivist and will be widely used for the foreseeable future, partially because of their predominant use throughout the world.

## Compression Tutorial

There are two types of compression used in image files, three if you count no compression.

**No Compression** – This format represents every pixel in exact detail, in a group of numbers in the image file. For the most common color format, it takes three bytes (or numbers) to record a single pixel. These three bytes represent the intensity of the three primary colors: Red, Blue, and Green (RGB).

**Lossless Compression** – This technique still maintains the detail for each pixel, but before the information is written to the image file, a mathematical formula reduces only the amount of numbers (bytes) that represent an image. For example, if an image contains a lot of white, black, or any same-color pixels, instead of writing each pixel dozens or hundreds of times, the mathematical reduction will record that fact that the next ten or 88 (or whatever number of occurrences) are all the same color.

Taking the 88 consecutive same-color pixels as an example, instead of writing three bytes for each one of the 88, the lossless algorithm needs to write only four bytes; three record the color, and one byte records how many of the next pixels use that color. This is determined as the image program reads the lines of pixels. There are several versions of this technique; the popular ZIP files use a variation.

Most programs that save TIF files offer the option of using LZW or ZIP. LZW is supported by most older software programs; this is the compression format I use.

**Lossy Compression** – While the term lossy is a made up non-word, it is descriptive, meaning the opposite of lossless. This compression technique loses image detail. But, why would you even want to reduce the detail?

Image compression reduces the size of the file. That is the only purpose of compression. Until recently, computer storage was very expensive, and disk capacity would quickly be used by large image files.

Compressed images are reduced in file size, requiring less disk space, therefore saving money. However, since technological advances continue to drive disk prices down and capacity up; file size is not as big of a concern – for storage purposes. Yet, large files can be cumbersome to send via email or backup to networks and cloud services. So small file size is still a viable goal, even though it has some penalties.

Without explaining the technical details, lossy compression averages similar, adjacent colors to a single color, requiring less information written to the file. This is usually not noticeable to most of us due to the tiny portion of the image that is affected. I offer a simple story that may help understand the results of compression.

This story uses an analogy of dog sounds, or sounds that only dogs can hear. While you and I cannot hear certain high-pitch frequencies, they still exist and dogs can hear them. Similarly, many times we cannot see a difference between a compressed picture (with reduced detail) and uncompressed picture. However, dogs can see it – no, they can't, just kidding. The detail image loss may be apparent to experts, noticed if the picture is enlarged, or if it has been compressed multiple times. Most times though, we do not notice it. JPG files use the type of lossy compression.

## Compression Example

This next picture is a high quality 5 x 7 photograph taken in 1925; it is a school picture and includes my father, second from the left in the front. The overall-clad boys and girls in flour-sack dresses were captured outside their single room school in rural Sumner County, Kansas.

1925 4" x 5" photograph (Bloody Run School, Sumner Co., Kansas)

The next table shows the relative affects of different types of file formats and compression. You will most often see the difference when examining a small portion of a photo, so I have zoomed in closely to the second boy on the left in the front row to view the differences. The Low Quality image shows pixelization, which creates a noticeably blurry image.

| TIFF (No Compression) | JPG (High Compression) | JPG (Low Compression) |
|:---:|:---:|:---:|
| 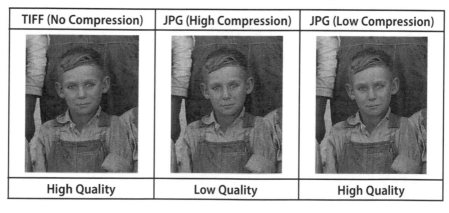 | | |
| High Quality | Low Quality | High Quality |

Center image shows pixelization from high compression.

## JPG Compression Settings

The JPG format allows users to set the compression level during the file-save process, which directly affects the image quality.

- High compression = lower quality images.
- Low compression = higher quality images.

Your scanner software (and image editing software) lets you change the setting, though different products use different terminology. This lack of non-standard terminology is confusing for many users. Some products use numbers, some use words to describe quality.

## Your Scanner's Settings

Each scanner brand will have a different menu and look, though the options will nearly always be the same, even with some terminology differences.

### General Settings

There are a variety of general settings you should verify when scanning. These include:

## Print or Film Scan?

You will need to select the kind of scan you are about to perform. The choices are to scan printed items (photographs) or transparent items (slides and negatives). Different scanners may use different terminology.

- Platen or Reflective is for photographs and documents.
- Film is for negatives and slides.

### Compression and Quality Settings

Compression and quality settings are usually referenced together. For our purpose of archiving slides and negatives always, use high quality settings with low compression.

Popular models of Canon and Epson scanners provide the following JPG settings.

| Scanner | Quality Setting |
|---|---|
| Canon 9000F | High (Low Compression)<br>Standard (Medium Compression)<br>Low (High Compression) |
| Epson V500 | 1 (High) – 100 (Low) |

These are representative settings for the two listed scanners. Other scanners may use different terminology that will accomplish the same objective.

## Understanding Resolution

When scanning negatives and slides you need to think in much higher resolution (DPI) terms than when scanning photographs. Think of the film as tiny photos. To arrive at viewable and printable images you need very high resolutions.

The following table gives recommended settings for different size negatives.

| Film Format | Minimum DPI | Standard DPI | Hi-Res DPI |
|---|---|---|---|
| 35mm | 1200 | 2400 | 3000 |
| 120 Film | 600 | 1200 | 2400 |
| 127 Film | 600 | 1200 | 2400 |
| 116 Film | 400 | 600 | 900 |
| 110 Film | 2400 | 3000 | 4000 |

Different film formats need different levels of DPI to produce a similar size image. For example, 35mm film is half the width of 120 format film; therefore, it needs to be scanned at twice the resolution to produce a similar size print image.

Tip – A Goldilocks setting, just right, would be the Standard DPI setting for the respective film format.

## Resolution Impact on Quality

We frequently hear and recommend that a good resolution for scanning objects is 300 DPI. That is true when the object is a normal or viewable size. For example, we would consider a postcard a normal size. A full page of paper would be normal size. If you scanned (or copied with a digital camera) one of these, a 300 DPI setting would let you reproduce a good quality picture at its original size.

300 DPI is a preferred resolution for most inkjet and laser printers, and photograph printing machines and services. However, scanning a small negative at 300 DPI will only give you a small picture the same size as the negative; this is not very useful.

When scanning very small photos, negatives, or slides you need to scan them at higher resolutions: 600, 1200, 2400, or even higher DPI settings. This will capture finer detail and allow you to enlarge the image to a size that is more pleasing to view.

## Now the DPI Confusion

DPI is an acronym for Dots Per Inch. This setting originally applied to print functions. Different printers could pack a different number of pixels into a physical inch of paper.

> Note – DPI vs. PPI: For use in this book DPI and PPI (Pixels Per Inch) are the same. They are becoming synonymous in the consumer world, though experts in digital arts will argue the differences ad-infinitum.

Printer or application software controlling the printer can set the resolution for the image to print – by reading the resolution value stored in the image.

This is where the confusion of DPI and resolution rears its ugly presence.

> DPI is an arbitrary and changeable setting ins every digital image.

If a 35mm negative is scanned at 1200 DPI, it will still print at its small size. However, if you change the resolution in an image editing program to 300 DPI, it will now print four times larger, making it a useful image.

## Resolution Example

I will explain the 35mm example. If you scan the negative at 300 DPI, it will print out at 1.4 inches wide, the size of the negative image since the file is set to 300 dots for one inch.

When you scan the same image a second time at 1200 DPI and immediately print it, the print will still be 1.4 inches wide because the file is telling the printer to put 1200 dots into one inch.

However, if you change this second file to 300 DPI – without resampling the image – and print it, the printed image will now be 5.2 inches wide as we are only putting 300 dots in an inch of paper. The picture is now four times larger. The image is spread out, but this is ok because we had so many dots to begin with: 1200. This action of changing the DPI did not affect the resolution of the file; it still has the same number of dots (pixels) from the 1200 DPI scan.

Note: The above example assumes you are not forcing the printer to override a specific size or resizing using a percentage.

Tip – You need to change the image resolution of your scanned file to 300 DPI after you scan the original at a higher setting.

Any good image editing software lets you change the resolution easily. See the software documentation or help section of your software.

## About Pixel and Printed Image Resolution

Pixel dimensions measure the total number of pixels along an image's width and height. Resolution is the fineness of detail in an image and is measured in pixels per inch (PPI or DPI). The more pixels per inch, the greater the resolution. Generally, an image with a higher resolution (more pixels) produces a better printed image quality.

Two rules are important to understanding image resolution and size:

- Image Resizing: Changes the size the image will print without changing the number of pixels in the image.
- Image Resampling: Changes the number of pixels in the image.

## Image Editing Software

**Picasa** – Picasa is a popular free image organizer and viewer from Google. While some adjustments and affects can be applied to images, it cannot be described as an image editor. Pixel-by-pixel editing and advanced formatting is not available. File saving formats are very limited, including the inability to save as TIF files.

**Photoshop Elements** – Is the younger sibling of the premier image editing software Photoshop. I am a user of both, with 25 years of Photoshop training and experience. The Elements version is a consumer-level product, but includes most of the same capabilities and features of the professional level version. Elements will do virtually any editing task you wish.

**Paint Shop Pro** – I used Paint Shop Pro for many years before migrating to Photoshop. Paint Shop Pro is a very capable editing program and will solve most consumer tasks.

**PhotoPlus** – This is a very capable yet unknown image editing program. If Elements and Paint Shop Pro did not exist I would use this program.

## Black & White or Color Scans

Even if you are scanning black and white negatives, set the scanner settings to color.

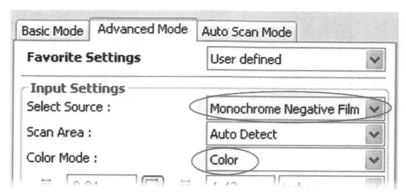

Source of scan is a black and white negative, but scanned in color.

One of the scanner color modes is called grayscale, a format that uses 256 shades of gray to represent an image. This may seem enough shades to represent a black and white image, however, a film negative may contain millions of shades; this is what makes many black and white images dynamic and beautiful.

Always scan in the color mode, even for black and white images. The basic color mode (RGB) uses 16.7 million colors. In a black and white image, they will all be gray (or some slight variation, depending on the scanner).

---

Tip – Always scan in the color mode, even when scanning black and white film. This rule of thumb also applies to scanning black and white photographic prints: Scan them in the color mode.

---

Do not confuse color mode with the source type. In this case, the source is black and white, but we want to scan using the color mode.

## Negative & Slide Holders

The scanners described in this book come with plastic templates that hold the film in place. These templates serve two purposes: First, they hold the film an optimized distance from the scanning sensors. Secondly, the film is held in a perfectly aligned position; that is the images are not crooked or leaning one way or the other.

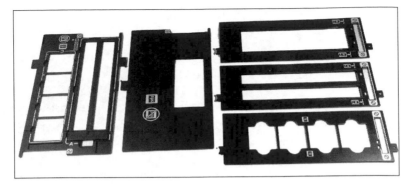

Variety of Epson and Canon film holders included with scanners.

These film holders accommodate 35mm negatives and slides, and 120 format negatives. The 120 format film has been in use since 1901 and is still available as it is the choice of many professionals. This format is commonly called medium format or 2¼ inch film, as it is 2¼ inches wide.

## Custom Negative Holders

Unfortunately, holders for 127 and 116 film sizes are not included, though these size negatives are commonly found in family archives. However, I do offer a solution for these shortcomings. You can make custom film holders from simple materials.

An APS (left) and 127 format (right) custom negative holder.

Instructions and templates for creating custom holders are included in Appendix C. The required materials include simple card stock or mat boards and tape. By following the exact dimensions and cutouts, perfect holders for odd-size negatives can be created easily.

These custom negative holders serve the same purpose as the plastic version supplied with the scanner.

## Placing Negative Directly on Glass

You can place oversize negatives directly on the scanner glass, though there are several disadvantage to this.

- Scanner focusing is optimized for the negatives to above the glass about 1.5 mm.
- It is difficult to keep the negative straight on the glass.
- The curl of the negative may cause movement when lid is closed.
- The curl (bow) of the negative may cause some portions to be out of focus.

Placing a negative on the scanner glass may be acceptable, even with the above difficulties, if your project only includes one or a couple negatives, or you just need a quick and less than archive quality scan. For any volume of odd-size negative scanning or if high-resolution archive quality scans are required, it is recommended you make one of the custom holders to fit your negative.

## Very Large Negatives

If you have very large negatives (including glass negatives) such as 4" x 5", 5" x 7" or even 8" x 10", a few extra steps are needed to arrive at a good scan; this includes stitching together multiple scans.

Tip – Scanning and stitching together very large negatives requires advanced expertise with image editing software. If you do not have this experience or the software, I recommend you have these scans performed by a professional.

A 4" x 5" negative next to a 120 format negative.

The negative scanning area of typical mid-range scanners will accommodate up to 120 format negatives, such as the smaller negative in the above image. Larger negatives such as the 4" x 5" negative need to be scanned in sections and then stitched together.

## Stitch Scans Together

Images can be stitched together using some advanced skills with a quality image editing program. Stitching images together is the process of merging two images of an adjacent scene resulting in a large image, ideally with no apparent seam or joint showing. This is required when scanning oversized negatives.

A variety of software packages have automated stitching routines, in addition to commands that allow you to manually merge multiple images. Follow your software documentation for stitching with your image editing application.

## Slide and Negative Scanner Components

First, a flatbed scanner technology discussion will help explain the scanning process. The scanner lights in the scanner lid of recommended scanners illuminate a maximum area 2¼" wide, the width of 120 format negatives, or maybe 2½" wide. These lights are specifically designed for transparent film and provide back-lighting that illuminates the negative (and slides). The same scanner sensors in the base of the machine that capture printed images also capture the negative image.

The trouble large negatives present is the illuminating lights in the lid may not cover the full width of large format film. This limitation requires scanning a large negative two or three times, each time moving a new portion of the negative into the lit area of the scanner. Then, the multiple images need to be stitched together.

## Scanning Large Negatives

I will use a 4" x 5" glass negative as an example of an oversized negative, scanning it twice to capture the complete image.

To easily and accurately stitch together two scans, you need each negative level when you scan it. It is easy to place the negative along the bottom (or top) edge of the scanner base, however some scanners do not scan to the edge. Also, it is helpful to have a guide such a ruler to align the negative.

If you have a short ruler, place it at the bottom edge of the scanner bed; a plastic one works best so you do not accidently scratch the scanner glass. Now lay the negative on the scanner bed, next to the ruler edge. An alternative is to use a piece of card stock paper, which allows you to place marks on it showing the available scanner area.

The next image shows a small ruler used as a guide while scanning. You can simply slide the negative from one side to another for multiple passes; noting the position on the ruler will help you determine how far to move the negative.

Preparing to scan a large negative with multiple passes.

After the first scan, move the remaining portion of the negative into the scan area. You can move it as much as you like, just be sure that some of the image you scanned in the first pass is ALSO viewable on the second pass. This overlap will help the stitching process.

You should now have two scans (or more for extremely large negatives) on your computer, each showing a portion of the large negative. Now you are ready to stitch the images together.

## Image Editing Tips – After Scanning

These tips may improve the beauty of your scans. They are usually accomplished using your image editing software.

- Reduce saturation to remove color from black and white images.
- Rotate image so it does not display at an angle.
- Crop your scan to eliminate excess area around the image.

*Photo Restoration KwikGuide*, a complete book on photo restoration by Gary W. Clark is available from Amazon.com. It is a step-by-step guide to enhancing photographs and repairing nearly any kind of damage. The Kwik-Guide includes a detailed chapter on Scanning and Copying, and a chapter on Straightening and Cropping your images; both of these are applicable to scanned slides and negatives.

## Advantages of Self-Scanning

- You can control the resolution.
- You can scan just a portion of an image.
- Eliminates sending film and slides away.
- Quicker turn-around time.

## Disadvantages of Self-Scanning

- Requires a good scanner with film & slide capabilities.
- Requires you to learn advanced scanner operations.
- You need to learn about resolution and compression.
- Lengthy time required to scan high number of images.

## Summary Steps to Great Scans

- Clean the scanner glass.
- Clean dust or other particles from negatives.
- Place negatives in holder and place on glass.
- Set scanner to correct negative source.
- Set scanner to scan in the color mode.
- Set scanner to appropriate resolution (DPI).
- Save image as TIF or high quality JPG files.

# 7

# SLIDE SCANNING – PERSONAL

This chapter covers 35mm slide scanning with your personal scanner connected to your home computer. Many commercial services are available and these were covered in Chapter 5 along with commercial negative scanning services.

Tip – If you have a large number of slides to scan, I recommend having them scanned by an inexpensive commercial service, even if you have a slide-capable scanner. This is much easier, and your slide images are returned on a CD. Scanning slides with your personal scanner can require a lot of time.

## Personal Scanning

The devices recommend in Chapter 6 on scanning negatives apply to slide scanners also. These consumer-level scanners are economical and easy to use, yet very capable of creating archival quality scans.

To recap, the scanners fall into three categories:

- Small, inexpensive, one-touch film scanners.
- Dedicated, expensive film scanners, for professional use.
- Flatbed scanner with special features for film scanning.

The third category, flatbed scanners, are again recommended for most family archiving projects.

Inexpensive one-touch, professional, and flatbed scanners.

## Your Flatbed Scanner

Many of the conditions and steps for scanning slides are the same for scanning negatives. Your scanner needs to have the capability to scan slides with specialized lights and slide templates; these are the same devices used for scanning negatives.

## Scanner Setup

The scanner mode needs to be set to match the type of scan; in this case, color positive film (slides). The setup window in the scanning software will provide a place to set the scanner for color slides.

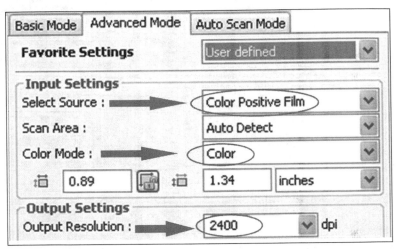

Choose 'Color Positive Film' for slides, and color for mode.

Besides the mode of scanning, you need to change the scanner resolution to 2400 DPI or greater. I recommend 2400 DPI for personal archiving. This will give you a nice size image with good detail.

If you wish to enlarge the slide to 8" x 10" or larger, choose a higher resolution; 3200 or 4800 will work fine, however the file size may become quite large. The above scanner setup window was from the Canon software with the 9000F scanner.

## Scanning Your Slides

### Slide Holders

Slide-ready scanners provide a template that holds the slides in place and ensures they are perfectly straight. Each template usually holds four slides, which means you can scan four slides at a time.

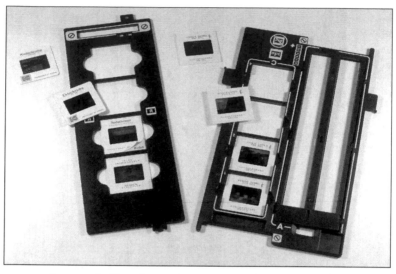

Cannon (left) and Epson (right) 35mm slide templates.

The Epson 35mm slide template (right) above is part of the 35mm negative holder also. Each brand or model of scanner comes with a specially designed holder; they are not interchangeable between scanners.

Most templates will hold four slides, but you do not have to scan four at once, a single slide can be inserted into the holder and scanned.

## Which Side of the Slide Is Up?

Slides (and negatives) can be laid on the scan glass with either side up. The difference in scan quality will not be apparent for family archiving. Even experts disagree on which side should face the scanning sensors.

However, if the slide is facing the wrong way, the image will be reversed. That is left will be right and right will be left. Any text or lettering in the image will be mirrored. A common, yet not fool proof, way to tell if a picture of adults has been reversed in scanning is to check which hand wedding rings are on.

The most common recommendation for most flatbed scanner is to place the emulsion side up. The emulsion side is where the actual chemical image of the film resides, and the film will have a dull surface. The other side of the slide (or film) will be shiny. Sometimes it is difficult to tell which side is dull or shiny; standing next to a light source and tilting the slide will usually give you an indication of dull versus shiny.

The shiny side usually includes the slide number and date.

An easier, and usually trustworthy, method of telling which side to lay on the scanner glass is to place the slide number down. Most slides were numbered and many were dated at production time. I have checked dozens of slides from the 1950s to the 1980s and found this rule was accurate 100% of the time.

Flatbed Scanners: Number and date on slide mount faces down (shiny side); emulsion side (dull) faces up.

Check words in the image to be sure they are correct and not reversed.
I took this photo of Mario Andretti at 1981 Road Race.

An exception to the rule applies to some bulk slide scanners. The Nikon slide scanner recommends the emulsion side should face the scanner sensors.

## Fixing a Backwards Slide

Most image editing software has a command that lets you flip or mirror the image.

- **Photoshop Elements**: The command can be found in IMAGE | ROTATE | FLIP HORIZONTAL.
- **Paint Shop Pro:** The command is IMAGE | FLIP HORIZONTAL.
- **Picasa**: There is an undocumented flip command in, CTRLSHFT-H.

Note, flipping is sometimes called mirroring.

## Summary Steps to Great Slide Scans

- Clean scanner glass.
- Clean dust or other particles from slides.
- Place slides in holder and place on glass.
- Set scanner source to Positive Film.
- Set scanner to scan in the color mode.
- Set scanner to ideal resolution (DPI), usually 2400.
- Save image as TIF or high quality JPG file.
- Return slide to a protective sleeve, tray, or box.

# ARCHIVING FOR FAMILY HISTORY

The information presented in this book described the physical preservation of vintage photographic negatives and slides. Yet, the tasks and work to save the images from the ravages of time and mishandling should serve the larger goal of understanding and weaving these images into family history publications, documents, and shared image libraries.

Share the photos with family and friends; and with like-minded people who may find them helpful in their own story telling. Photographs are visual stories. Do not let these stories pass with time; they are history that should be remembered and retold over and over again.

Gary W. Clark

# NOTES

1   Yale University Library, Preservation Department, Identification of Film Types, August 2011.

2   Northeast Document Conservation Center, A Short Guide to Film Base Photographic Materials, 2007, 2012.

3   Kodak, Storage and Handling of Processed Nitrate Film.

4   Kodak, Article Information Sheet, 2003, http://www.kodak.com/ek/US/en/About_Kodak_Top/Global_Sustainability/Material_Safety_Data_Sheets.htm.

5   United Nations Educational, Scientific and Cultural Organization, Main principles of fire protection in libraries and archives: A RAMP study, 1992.  http://www.unesco.org/webworld/ramp/html/r9214e/r9214e04.htm.

6   Association of Moving Image Archivists, Identifying and Handling Nitrate Film, 2008, http://www.amianet.org/groups/committees/nitrate/documents/NitrateIGNov08.pdf.

7.  Kodak Slide Projectors, http://slideprojector.kodak.com/archives/chronology.shtml.

8.  Photographic Solutions: http://photosol.com/product/pec-12-4-oz/.

9.  Library of Congress, Recommended Format Specifications 2014-2015, http://www.loc.gov/preservation/resources/rfs/rfs20142015.pdf.

# NEGATIVE FORMATS AND SIZES

| # | Type | Introduced | Stopped | Image Size |
|---|------|-----------|---------|-----------|
| 101 | Roll Film | 1895 | 1956 | 3½" × 3½" |
| 102 | Roll Film | 1896 | 1933 | 1½" × 2" |
| 103 | Roll Film | 1896 | 1949 | 3¾" × 4¾" |
| 104 | Roll Film | 1897 | 1949 | 4¾" × 3¾" |
| 105 | Roll Film | 1897 | 1949 | 2¼" × 3¼" |
| 106 | Roll Film | 1898 | 1924 | 3½" × 3½" |
| 107 | Roll Film | 1898 | 1924 | 3¼" × 4¼" |
| 108 | Roll Film | 1898 | 1929 | 4¼" × 3¼" |
| 109 | Roll Film | 1898 | 1924 | 4" × 5" |
| 111 | Roll Film | 1898 | ? | 6½" × 4¾" |
| 112 | Roll Film | 1898 | 1924 | 7" × 5" |
| 113 | Roll Film | 1898 | ? | 9 × 12 cm |
| 114 | Roll Film | 1898 | ? | 12 × 9 cm |
| 115 | Roll Film | 1898 | 1949 | 6¾" × 4¾" |
| 116 | Roll Film | 1899 | 1984 | 2½" × 4¼" |
| 117 | Roll Film | 1900 | 1949 | 2¼" × 2¼" |
| 118 | Roll Film | 1900 | 1961 | 3¼" × 4¼" |
| 119 | Roll Film | 1900 | 1940 | 4¼" × 3¼" |
| 120 | Roll Film | 1901 | Present | 2¼" × 2¼" |
| 122 | Roll Film | 1903 | 1971 | 3¼" × 5½" |
| 123 | Roll Film | 1904 | 1949 | 4" × 5" |
| 125 | Roll Film | 1905 | 1949 | 3¼" × 2½" x 2 |
| 124 | Roll Film | 1905 | 1961 | 3¼" × 4¼" |
| 126 | Roll Film | 1906 | 1949 | 4¼" x 6½" |
| 126 | Cartridge | 1963 | 2008 | 28.5 x 28.5 mm |
| 128 | Roll Film | 1912 | 1941 | 1½" × 2¼" |
| 129 | Roll Film | 1912 | 1951 | 1 5/8" × 3" |

# ARCHIVAL STANDARDS

Archival standards are published by a number of agencies, institutions, and associations. Many of these specifications are ideal conditions for professional storage facilities, and may vary slightly.

## Storage Environment Specifications

### National Archives:

Temperature: 65° - 70° F

Humidity: 35 – 50%

### Library of Congress (LOC):

Temperature: Room temperature or below

Humidity: 30 – 40%

Light: Minimal Light

## Home Environment Standards

For the home archivist, these are ideal guidelines, though difficult or impractical to achieve at home. Extreme conditions outside of the specifications may be detrimental to your archives.

### Conditions to AVOID:

- Storage in a garage or basement with no climate control.
- Storage in an unfinished attic with no climate control.
- Storage in a detached building with no climate control.
- Open container storage, especially in high humidity.
- Storage in direct sunlight or bright artificial light.
- Storage in low areas prone to flooding (basements).
- Storage near plumbing or other water sources.

## Acceptable Storage & Display Products

### Sterilite Storage Containers

The Sterilite web page lists their products as polypropylene and polyethylene. No PVC content and are acid-free. (www.sterilite.com/general_info.html). These are handy clear containers found in major discount stores. Note: They do not recommend storing negatives in them.

### Rubbermaid Storage Containers

Many plastic containers by Rubbermaid and found in most discount stores are acid-free and suitable for archival storage. See the section below on Storage Containers.

### Archival Boxes

Special acid-free, lignin-free storage available from archival specialty companies.

### Baseball Card Sleeves

Made from polypropylene, name brand sleeves are acid-free and archival save. See the vendor list in previous appendix.

## Products to Avoid

### PVC Products

Seldom found now for archiving, do not use PVC-based storage containers. Most tubes and pipes are PVC, do not use to store rolled documents. Older sheet protectors that have turned yellow and brittle probably contain PVC.

### Magnetic Photo Albums

These are not magnetic, but use a sticky chemical to hold pictures in place. Do not use.

### Shoe Boxes or Other Retail Packaging

The original boxes your shoes came in are cheaply made and the cardboard most likely contains acids and lignin.

## Acid-Free Storage Containers

Many household storage containers are acid-free and lignin free. Most are made of polypropylene which is used widely in archival products. As pointed out above, Sterilite has an archival statement on their website.

We contacted Rubbermaid, asking for a statement on archival safe containers. The following is the response received from Rubbermaid on October 9, 2013.

> *"Our products are house wares and as such have not been tested for archival properties so we can't recommend them for specific preservation applications. However, most of our storage type products considered for such use are made of polyethylene, polypropylene, polystyrene which contain no plasticizers. Archivists avoid materials like PVC (vinyl) due to the presence of these additives. The recycle code molded into the bottom of each item identifies the family. It is a triangle with a number inside and letters along the bottom. This code indicates the material from which the product is made." - Rubbermaid Consumer Service*

Their recommendations are in line with standard practices. The codes referred to are stamped on the bottom of many containers, including Sterilite and Rubbermaid brands.

---

Note: The term 'Acid-free' is used frequently throughout this book and in most archive writing. Acids are a natural by-product of most plants, including wood as the plant breaks down. Acids can also be introduced into a product during manufacturing. Acids have deteriorating affects on most tobjects. The most common damage we see is document yellowing. This damage can come from the acid in the document itself, for example yellowed and brittle newsprint, or contact with an object with acid content.

---

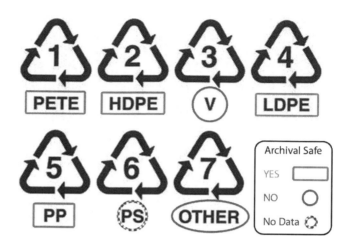

Industry chart of plastic codes.

We annotated the chart to highlight the good product codes (square) and the ones to avoid (oval). Polyvinylchloride plastics (3) are the most dangerous ones to avoid. Code 6 is a dotted circle because there is little data on this kind of plastic used in containers. Here is a recap of the codes, in plain English

1. PETE - Polyethylene terephthalate (polyester)
2. HDPE - High density polyethylene
3. V – Polyvinyl chloride (PVC)
4. LDPE - Low density polyethylene
5. PP - Polypropylene
6. PS - Polystyrene
7. OTHER - All others

A note for long term storage. Formal, archival-safe boxes are made of organic products that do not seal tightly. The boxes breath, allowing air to circulate which prevents mold. Plastic containers with tight lids could promote fungal growth if moisture is trapped inside.

Drill a few small holes in the side of the container, just below the lid. This still lets the container protect the contents from any wet flooring.

## Archival Definitions

### PAT – ANSI Photographic Activity Test.

Note: The following two paragraphs are from the Image Permanence Institute website: https://www.imagepermanenceinstitute.org/testing/pat

The Photographic Activity Test, or PAT, is an international standard test (ISO18916) for evaluating photo-storage and display products. Developed by IPI, this test explores interactions between photographic images and the enclosures in which they are stored.

The PAT is routinely used to test papers, adhesives, inks, glass and framing components, sleeves, labels, photo albums, scrapbooking supplies and embellishments, as well as other materials upon request.

### Lignin Free

Lignin is a chemical in wood-based products (paper) that breaks down and becomes acidic.

### PH Neutral

PH is a scale of acid to alkaline. For archival purposes it refers to the acid (or lack of) in paper products. The scale runs from zero (high acidity) to 14, high alkaline, with seven being neutral. All acid-free materials have a PH of seven (7) or above

### Acid-free

Acid-free means the product has no acid in it, which causes damage to documents and photographs. Acid-free applies to paper, storage boxes, envelopes, labels, and markers. Acid causes paper and paper products to deteriorate. A common example is newsprint, which has very high acid content.

### Polyvinylchloride (PVC)

PVC is generally found in industrial and construction products, though some tubes, mats, toys, and computer parts are made of PVC. Also, disposable packaging including bottles and blister packs may be PVC. Do not re-use for archival purposes. Also, do not store PVC products with archived objects. PVC gives off gas.

## Polypropylene

An acid-free clear material suitable for document and photograph storage. Typically base ball type sleeves protectors are an example.

## Polyethylene

Also used in some sleeve protectors, it is equally safe as polypropylene, though usually not as clear.

## Polyvinyl Chloride (PVC)

An industrial plastic used in pipes, flooring, signs, electrical insulation, and some upholstery. PVC degrades easily and gives off gases harmful to archived objects. Old sheet protectors that have turned yellow and brittle should be replaced.

# CUSTOM NEGATIVE TEMPLATES

Blueprints and instructions for constructing custom templates for odd-size negatives are provided for the following negative formats:

- APS Format Negatives
- 110 Format Negatives
- 127 Format Negatives
- 116 Format Negatives
- 122 Format Negatives

The templates are each constructed of three pieces of mat or backing board. The designs provide 1) a bottom piece that supports the negative, 2) a center piece provides a well that keeps the negative in position, and 3) a top cover flattens the negative and keeps it in place for scanning.

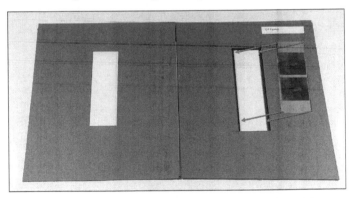

Custom templates hold the negative flat and straight.

These templates are made from backing cardboard that are placed behind pictures during framing. This material can be found in art, framing, crafts, and hobby stores. Mat boards are attractive and function well, though they are too thick to cut easily. Common card stock is generally too thin to provide the stiffness needed for some heavily curled negatives.

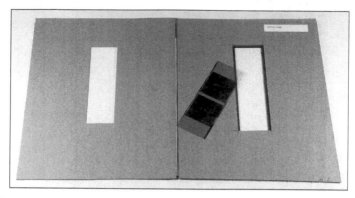

Easy to us templates sized for each negative make scanning easy.

A PDF file for each negative size is available on the Phototree website; providing a sample layout with dimensions needed to create the template.

**Download templates: www.phototree.com/templates.htm**

# GLOSSARY

### Acid-free
If an object is labeled acid-free, acid that naturally occurred in the material was removed, or none was introduced during the manufacturing process. One of the most common traits of acid in paper is yellowing.

### Cellulose Acetate
A compound made from cotton or wood pulp fibers and acetate. An early synthetic compound, it replaced cellulose nitrate as a photograph film base, become known as Safety Film. Cellulose acetate is stable, though deterioration will emit a vinegar odor.

### Conservator
A trained expert in the physical restoration of items such as paintings, books, textiles, photographs, documents, and other objects. The American Institute for Conservation of Historic and Artistic Works (AIC) provides guidance in finding a conservator. See their website at http://www.conservation-us.org/home.

### Flatbed Scanner
A desktop scanner for scanning documents and photographs. Newer flatbed scanners have built-in capabilities to scan negatives and slides.

### Glass Plate Negative
Glass plates were used from the 1860s until the early 1900s as the negative base. The glass was coated with light sensitive chemicals that became the image when exposed to light.

### Lignin
Lignin is a natural occurring substance in plants and wood. It is an integral part of transferring water through the plant. Upon breaking down

after the plant has died, it becomes an acid which is hazardous to paper
and photographs.

### Nitrate (Cellulose Nitrate, Nitrocellulose, Guncotton)

Early film negatives and movie film made from nitrate cellulose which is
hazardous and highly flammable.

### Polyester

A chemical compound that became the foundation of millions of objects including clothes. It also became the film-base choice beginning in
the 1980s, replacing cellulose acetate.

### Positive (Transparency)

A viewable likeness on film, not a negative.

### Safety Film

See cellulose acetate.

# BOOKS BY GARY W. CLARK

## KwikGuide Series

### Photo Restoration KwikGuide

A Step-by-Step Guide for Repairing Photographs with Photoshop Elements

### 19th Century Card Photos KwikGuide

A Step-by-Step Guide to Identifying and Dating Cartes de Visite and Cabinet Cards

### Cased Images and Tintypes KwikGuide

A Guide to Identifying and Dating Daguerreotypes, Ambrotypes, and Tintypes

### Real Photo Postcards KwikGuide

A Guide to Identifying and Dating Real Photo Postcards of the 20th Century

## Home Archivist Series

### Archive Photography

How to photograph oversize photos, curled documents, and heirloom treasures.

### Gravestone Photography and Documentation

Document ancestor graves with photographs and location data.

### Slides and Negatives

Digitizing and Protecting Your Vintage Film

These books are available from Amazon.com in print and Kindle format.

## Photograph Research Website

PhotoTree.com provides a wealth of history and identification tips on its free website, along with a gallery of 1,000 images and case studies.

For vintage photo information resource visit: http://www.phototree.com.

## Video Channel

The PhotoTree channel on YouTube delivers revealing videos of film-burn tests conducted by PhotoTree. These include dramatic flash fires of nitrate films along with tests on acetate and modern polyester films. These videos can be found at www.phototree.com/burn.htm.

## Product Reviews

All products used and described in this book have been tested by PhotoTree. com. For descriptions, reviews, and sources visit our Product Review Page (www.phototree.com/links_products1.htm).

## Book Reviews

If you have the time, a review of this book would be appreciated on the Amazon webpage for this book. Other readers may be interested in your honest opinion of the book. Thank you.

## Author Biography

I am a professional photographer, graphics designer, and genealogist who has merged those pursuits and now share the information, techniques, and skills I have learned with others. My author page on Amazon.com tells of current interests, activities, and new publications and can be reached at: www.amazon.com/author/gary-clark

23084810R00063

Made in the USA
Middletown, DE
16 August 2015